The Cat in the Hat's Learning Library

The editors would like to thank
BARBARA KIEFER, Ph.D.,
Charlotte S. Huck Professor of Children's Literature,
The Ohio State University, and
PAUL L. SIESWERDA,
Aquarium Curator, New York Aquarium,
for their assistance in the preparation of this book.

www.randomhouse.com/kids
www.seussville.com

Library of Congress Cataloging-in-Publication Data
Worth, Bonnie.
A whale of a tale! : all about porpoises, dolphins, and whales / by Bonnie Worth ; illustrated by
Aristides Ruiz and Joe Mathieu. — 1st ed.
    p.   cm. — (Cat in the Hat's learning library)
Includes index.
ISBN 0-375-82279-8 (trade) — ISBN 0-375-92279-2 (lib. bdg.)
1. Porpoises—Juvenile literature. 2. Dolphins—Juvenile literature.
3. Whales—Juvenile literature. I. Ruiz, Aristides. II. Mathieu, Joseph. III. Title. IV. Series.
QL737.C434W67 2006
599.5—dc22
2005000616

Printed in the United States of America   First Edition   10 9 8 7 6 5 4 3 2 1
RANDOM HOUSE and colophon are registered trademarks of Random House, Inc.

A Whale of a Tale!

by Bonnie Worth

illustrated by Aristides Ruiz and Joe Mathieu

The Cat in the Hat's Learning Library™

Random House 🏠 New York

What's the story today?
Funny that you should ask.
We're going to take on
a whale of a task:
to learn about whales
and their smaller relations,
porpoises and dolphins—
the group called cetaceans
(sih-TAY-shunz).

So please hang on tight as
we lower down toward
the boat that we soon
will be sailing aboard.
One very large boat,
the best in the nation—
Captain McElligot's
Cetacean Station!

Like monkeys and donkeys,
and dogs, cats, and camels,
whales, porpoises, and dolphins
are all kinds of mammals.

Cetaceans might look
like the fish in the sea,
but cetaceans are closer
to you and to me.
They're warm-blooded, like us,
but with fins and no legs.
They give birth to live babies
and do not lay eggs.

ADULT PYGMY RIGHT WHALE

EGGS

Fish breathe through gills,
like that cod over there,

GILLS

8

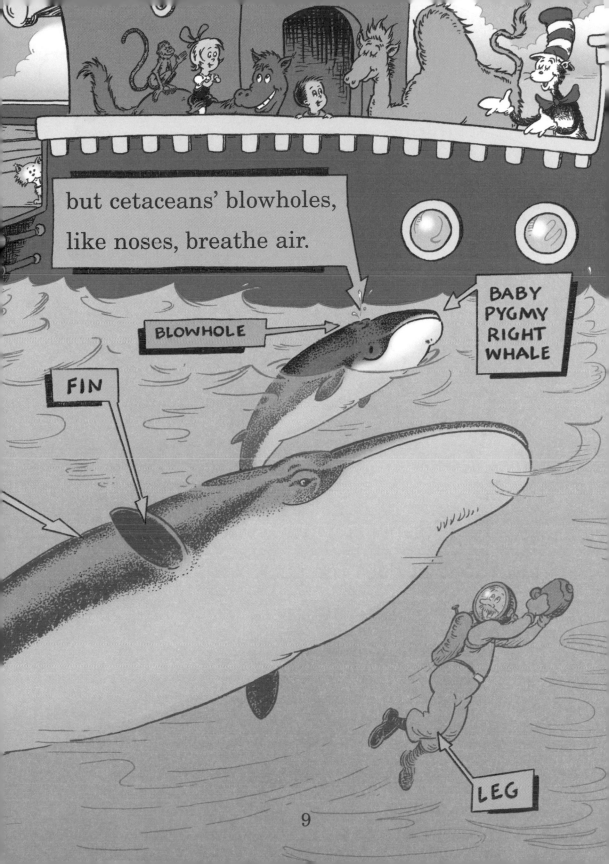

but cetaceans' blowholes,
like noses, breathe air.

BLOWHOLE

BABY
PYGMY
RIGHT
WHALE

FIN

LEG

9

Land mammals have bodies
all covered with hairs.
Cetaceans have just a few
spare hairs on theirs.

Our hair keeps us warm,
but their fat does the trick.
Sometimes, like a mattress,
it's two whole feet thick!

BLUBBER

10

Another big difference between whales and fish— Thing One and Thing Two can explain, if you wish:

Fish flap their tails side to side when they go.

FISH TAIL

But whales flip theirs upward and downward like so!

WHALE TAIL

Some cetaceans catch food
with the teeth in their head.
Others use something
called baleen instead.

TEETH

BALEEN

KRILL

Baleen grows in rows
and forms sort of a grill
for straining the tiny
sea critters called krill.

RIGHT WHALE

But toothed or baleen,
cetaceans don't chew.
They swallow food whole.
That's all that they do.

TOOTHED WHALES

SPOTTED DOLPHIN

GULF PORPOISE

KILLER WHALE or ORCA

Some whales even swallow
some things by mistake:
a bucket, a boot, or
a big rubber snake.

SPERM WHALE

13

Most cetaceans we know
like to swim in a troop.
A pod is the name that
we give to this group.

FALSE
KILLER
WHALES

If danger is near, they
will sound an alert
to keep their young safe and
help those who are hurt.

Because it is smallish,
the porpoise is shy.
It swims near the shore
and does not leap up high.

Only Dall's porpoise
swims out in the sea—
thirty miles an hour,
the porpoise speedy!

We can all play a game.

So let's make a start:

PORPOISE OR DOLPHIN?—

who can tell them apart?

Porpoise teeth are flat.
Dolphins' are cones.
Porpoise noses are shorter,
with delicate bones.

Porpoise or dolphin?
It's easy to spot.
Dolphins' noses are long,
but porpoises' are not.

D.

E.

A. SPOTTED DOLPHIN
B. FINLESS
PORPOISE
C. SPECTACLED
PORPOISE
D. COMMON
DOLPHIN
E. BOTTLENOSE
DOLPHIN

Of dolphins, there are
about thirty-five types.
Some dolphins have patches
and others have stripes.

RISSO'S
DOLPHIN

FRASER'S
DOLPHIN

SHORT-BEAKED
COMMON
DOLPHIN

These markings are really
a very good way
of hiding the dolphins
as they hunt their prey.

The smallest is five feet
from its nose to its tail.
The largest is orca,
or the killer whale.

ORCA

HECTOR'S
DOLPHIN

Bottlenose leaps forward
as neat as you please.

The dusky leaps backward
and does it with ease.

The one we call spinner,
McElligot knows,
spins round in the air—
like a top, this guy goes!

And sometimes the spinner
will come to a stop
and peer out of the water.
It's called a "spyhop."

INDO-PACIFIC HUMPBACK
DOLPHIN

This humpback is one very
odd-looking mammal.
Its back has a hump
like the land-living camel.

This dolphin's a boto,
and what would you think
if I told you the boto
has skin that is pink?

BOTO

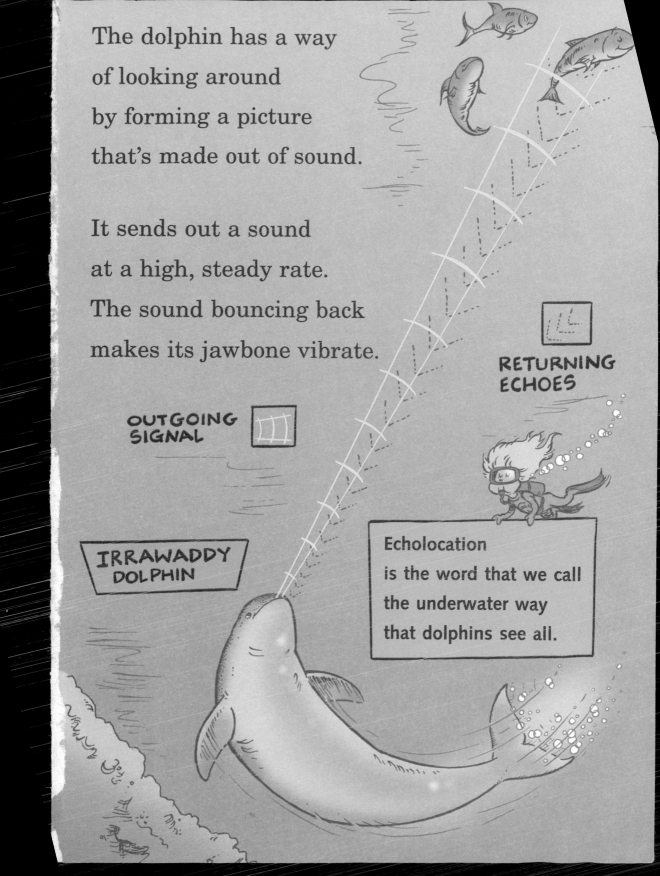

The dolphin has a way
of looking around
by forming a picture
that's made out of sound.

It sends out a sound
at a high, steady rate.
The sound bouncing back
makes its jawbone vibrate.

OUTGOING
SIGNAL

RETURNING
ECHOES

IRRAWADDY
DOLPHIN

Echolocation
is the word that we call
the underwater way
that dolphins see all.

Most dolphins could win
Mommy of the Year.
They care for their young
and keep them quite near.
    When dolphins are born,
    a nurse dolphin is there
    to bring baby up
    to breathe in its first air.

And when mom goes to hunt,
why, this thoughtful critter
leaves baby behind
with the babysitter!

I bet you are thinking—
hey, what about whales?
The biggest comes last.
(Oh, that trick never fails!)

SEI WHALES

Whales, as a rule,
like to stay on the move,
as all of our studies
can easily prove.

28

In tropical seas
in the winter, they breed.
In the summer, they swim
toward the poles to feed.

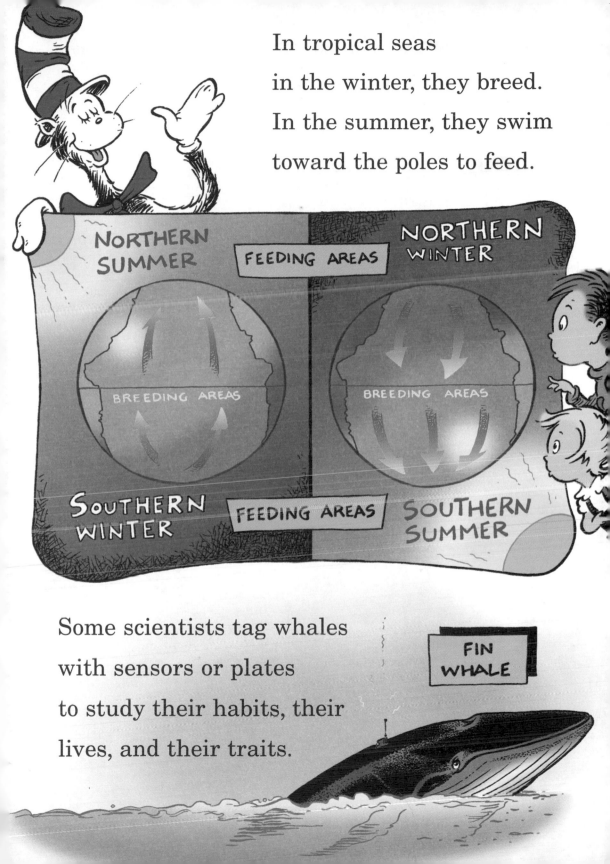

NORTHERN SUMMER

FEEDING AREAS

NORTHERN WINTER

BREEDING AREAS

BREEDING AREAS

SOUTHERN WINTER

FEEDING AREAS

SOUTHERN SUMMER

Some scientists tag whales
with sensors or plates
to study their habits, their
lives, and their traits.

FIN WHALE

The sperm whale can dive
down one mile or more.
Its rich blood and muscles
are up to the chore.

SPERM WHALE

A cave in its head
that's the size of a jeep
weighs down the whale's body
and helps it sink deep.

31

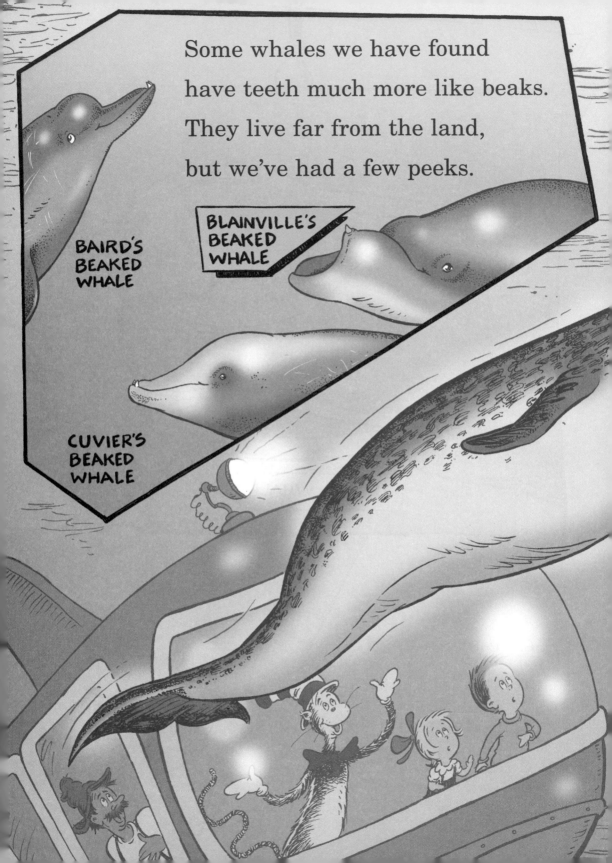

Some whales we have found
have teeth much more like beaks.
They live far from the land,
but we've had a few peeks.

BAIRD'S
BEAKED
WHALE

BLAINVILLE'S
BEAKED
WHALE

CUVIER'S
BEAKED
WHALE

The narwhal's long tooth
is a tusk, as you see.
It might work as a sword.
Or an ice pick, maybe?

One day you might hear
a big and loud SPLASH!!
A whale has leapt up
and come down with a CRASH!!!

We call this act breaching,
and no person—not one!—
knows why the whales do this.
Perhaps just for fun?

The best breachers of all
are these whales, they say:
humpback and sperm,
right whale and gray.

GRAY WHALE

HUMPBACK
WHALE

SPERM WHALE

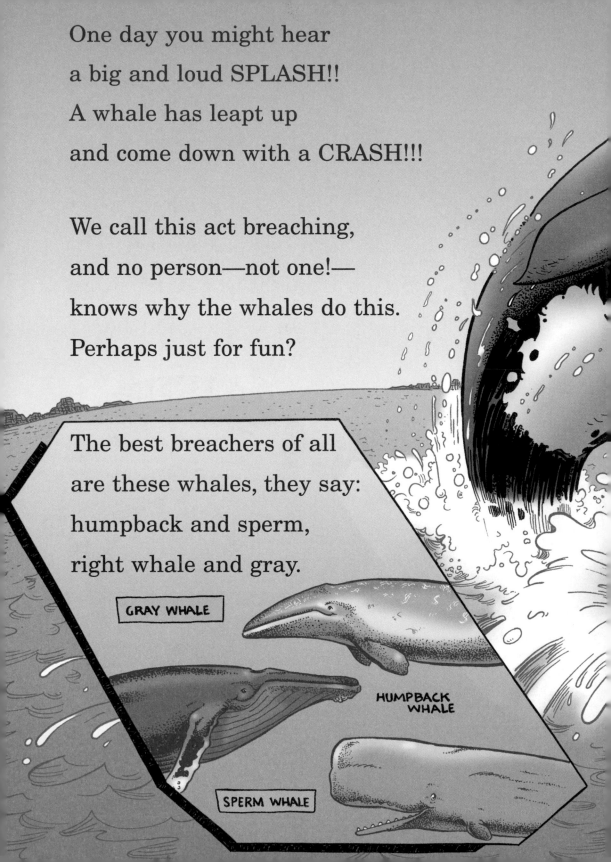

The ocean is loud with the
sounds of whales talking,
their clicking and groaning
and moaning and squawking.

Why is it whales talk?
To communicate!
Who, what, why, and where,
and if they'll be late.

36

The humpback's sweet song won McElligot's heart. It even showed up on the pop music chart!

Dick and Sally, all set?
Oh, this will be a blast.
Here comes the blue whale.
The biggest comes last!

MOM WHALE
LENGTH—
84 FEET
WEIGHT—
120 TONS

The blue whale is BIG,
and for what it is worth,
it's the biggest thing
living in sea or on earth!

The blue whale is big.

Yes, indeed, and what's more,

bigger still than the big,

BIG,

BIG,

BIGGEST

DINOSAUR!

The story of the porpoise,
the dolphin, and the whale,
you have to admit . . .

. . . is a whale of a tale!

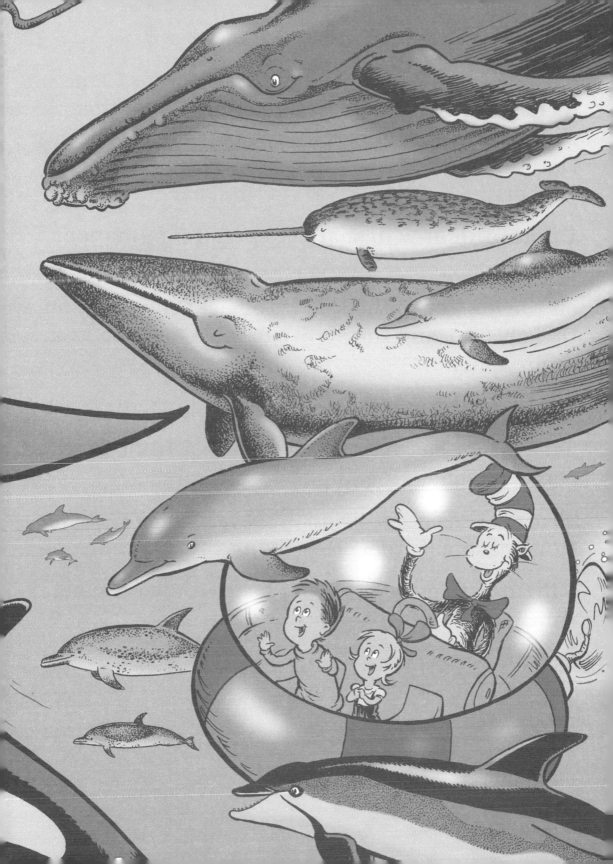

GLOSSARY

Cetaceans: Water mammals of the order Cetacea, including dolphins, porpoises, and whales, that share common features like nearly hairless bodies; flat, (usually) notched tails; and arm-like front flippers.

Communicate: To share or spread information.

Mammals: Warm-blooded animals, living either on the land or in the sea, with backbones, hair on their bodies, and the ability to make milk to feed their young.

Sensors: Devices that can read a signal.

Straining: Passing through a net or filter to separate solids from liquids.

Traits: The details or qualities that make a living thing different from other living things.

Vibrate: To move back and forth at a very rapid rate.

FOR FURTHER READING

Do Whales Have Belly Buttons? Questions and Answers About Whales and Dolphins by Melvin Berger and Gilda Berger, illustrated by Higgins Bond (Scholastic). Easy-to-read questions and answers about cetaceans. For ages 4 and up.

Dolphins! by Sharon Bokoske, illustrated by Richard Courtney (Random House, *Step into Reading,* Step 3). Fascinating facts about dolphin anatomy, social groups, and intelligence. For ages 4 and up.

Splash! A Book About Whales and Dolphins by Melvin Berger and Gilda Berger (Cartwheel Books, *Hello Reader! Science,* Level 3). Full-color photos illustrate this introduction to the watery world of whales and dolphins. For ages 4 and up.

Whales by Gallimard Jeunesse and Claude Delafosse, illustrated by Ute Fuhr and Raoul Sautai (Scholastic, *A First Discovery Book*). All about different kinds of whales. Transparent pages show whales from different angles—and one reveals the animal's skeletal system! For ages 4 and up.

INDEX

air, 9, 22, 26

Baird's beaked whale, 32
baleen, 12, 13
Blainville's beaked whale, 32
blowholes, 9
blubber, 10
blue whales, 38–39, 40
boto dolphins, 24
bottlenose dolphins, 19, 22
breaching, 34–35
breathing, 8, 9
breeding, 29

camels, 8, 24
care of young, 26–27
cats, 8
cetaceans, 6, 8, 9, 10, 12
cod, 8
common dolphins, 19
communication, 36–37
Cuvier's beaked whale, 32

Dall's porpoise, 17
danger, 14
dinosaurs, 39

dogs, 8, 10
dolphins, 6, 8, 18, 19, 20–27, 39, 40, *see also* individual species
donkeys, 8
dusky dolphins, 22

earth (land), 38
echolocation, 25
eggs, 8

false killer whales, 14–15
fat, *see* blubber
feeding, 12–13, 20, 29
fin whales, 29
finless porpoises, 18–19
fins, 8, 9
fish, 8, 11
Fraser's dolphin, 20

gray whales, 34
groups, 14
gulf porpoises, 13

hairs, 10
Hector's dolphin, 21
humpback whales, 34, 36–37, 41

Indo-Pacific humpback
    dolphins, 24
Irrawaddy dolphins, 25

keeping warm, 10
killer whales, 12, 13, 21,
    40
krill, 12

legs, 8, 9

mammals, 8, 9, 10, 24
markings, 20
migration, 29
monkeys, 8

narwhals, 32–33, 41
noses, 9, 19, 21

orca, *see* killer whales

pods, 14
porpoises, 6, 8, 16–17, 18,
    19, 39, *see also*
    individual species
pygmy right whales, 8–9

right whales, 12, 34–35

Risso's dolphin, 20

scientists, 29
seas, 8, 29, 38
sei whales, 28
sharks, 14–15
short-beaked common
    dolphins, 20
spectacled porpoises,
    18–19
sperm whales, 13, 30–31,
    34
spinner dolphins, 22–23
spotted dolphins, 13,
    18–19
"spyhop," 22
summer, 29
swimming, 11, 14–15, 16,
    17, 28, 29, 30, 34–35

tails, 11, 21
teeth, 12, 13, 19, 32, 33

whales, 6, 8, 11, 13, 28–39,
    40, *see also* individual
    species
winter, 29